Voices
of the
Dream

African-American Women Speak

Edited by Venice Johnson

CHRONICLE BOOKS

SAN FRANCISCO

Page 106 is considered a continuation of this copyright page.

Book and cover design by Pamela Geismar

Printed in Singapore

Library of Congress Cataloging-in-Publication Data:
Voices of the dream : African-American Women Speak / edited by Venice Johnson
          p.   cm.
      Includes bibliographical references.
      Summary: Quotations by notable African-American women are accompanied by reproductions of paintings, drawings, and mixed-media artworks by contemporary African-American women artists.
          ISBN 0-8118-1113-1
      1. Afro-American women—Quotations—Juvenile literature. 2. Afro-American art—Juvenile literature. [1. Afro-American women—Quotations. 2. Afro-American art.] I. Johnson, Venice.
          PN6081.3.V35   1996
          081'.08996—dc20   95-18941
                                                         CIP   AC

Distributed in Canada by
Raincoast Books
8680 Cambie Street
Vancouver, B.C. V6P 6M9

10 9 8 7 6 5 4 3 2 1

Chronicle Books
275 Fifth Street
San Francisco, CA 94103

The true worth of a race must be measured
by the character of its womanhood. . . .

Mary McLeod Bethune

My Right As a Future of Equality with Other Americans   *Elizabeth Catlett*

9 x 6", color linocut. 1947. Courtesy of the artist.

We don't have an eternity to realize
our dreams, only the time we are here.

Susan Taylor

I am not going to die, I'm going home
like a shooting star.

Sojourner Truth

I am where I am because of the bridges
that I crossed. Sojourner Truth was
a bridge. Harriet Tubman was a bridge.
Ida B. Wells was a bridge. Madame
C. J. Walker was a bridge. Fannie Lou
Hamer was a bridge.   *Oprah Winfrey*

Josephine Baker

My greatest desire will always be to see
my people happier in this country.

The Sunflower Quilting Bee at Arles *Faith Ringgold*

24 x 22", pastel and collage. 1995. Courtesy of the artist.

Strong people don't need strong leaders.

Ella Baker

I knew that whatever I set my mind to do, I could do.

Wilma Rudolph

Our skins may differ, but from thee we claim
A sister's privilege and a sister's name.

Sarah Forten

I'm just the same as I was before you
knew I was colored and just the same
afterwards. Why should it ever have
made any difference at all?

Jesse Redmon Fauset

Shaded Lives *Phoebe Beasley*

40 x 30", collage. 1988. Collection of Alex Gallery, Washington, D.C.

40 x 30", oil. 1993. Courtesy of the artist.

Maria W. Stewart

O, ye daughters of Africa, awake! . . . ye are
endowed with noble and exalted faculties.

On my underground railroad, I never
ran my train off the track, and I never
lost a passenger.

Harriet Tubman

People don't pay much attention
to you when you are second best.
I wanted to see what it felt like to
be number one.

Florence Griffith Joyner

I knew we had no aviators, neither
men nor women, and I knew the race
needed to be represented . . . so I
thought it my duty to risk my life to
learn aviation and encourage flying
among men and women of our race.

Bessie Coleman

Ida B. Wells

> We must do something and we must
> do it now. We must educate the white
> people out of their two hundred fifty
> years of slave history.

. . . to be a colored woman is to be
discredited, mistrusted, and often
meanly hated.

Fannie Barrier Williams

Autobiography: Fire: Suttee   *Howardena Pindell*

90 x 56", Acrylic, paper, polymer photo transfer on canvas. Copyright © Howardena Pindell, 1986-87.
Collection of Peter Huber, Norfolk, Virginia.

Mt. Pilgrim Baptist Church   *Marie Johnson Calloway*

96 x 124", mixed media. 1968–85. Courtesy of the artist.

'Twant me, 'twas the Lord. I always
told Him, "I trust you. I don't know
where to go or what to do, but I expect
you to lead me." And He always did.

Harriet Tubman

One isn't necessarily born with courage,
but one is born with potential. Without
courage, we cannot practice any other
virtue with consistency. We can't be kind,
true, merciful, generous, or honest.

Maya Angelou

For I am my mother's daughter, and the drums of Africa still beat in my heart. They will not let me rest while there is a single Negro boy or girl without a chance to prove his worth.

Mary McLeod Bethune

Who can be born black and not exult!   *Mari Evans*

Flight *Irmagean*

Midnight Rendezvous/Night Kiss   *Margo Humphrey*

22 x 30", color lithograph. 1989. Collection of United States Information Agency, Arts America Program, Washington, D.C.

Or maybe the purpose of being here,
wherever we are, is to increase the
durability and the occasions of love
among and between peoples. Love,
as the concentration of tender caring
and tender excitement, or love as the
reason for joy. . . . Love is the single,
true prosperity of any moment and
that whatever and whoever impedes,
diminishes, ridicules, opposes
the development of loving spirit is
"wrong"/hateful.   *June Jordan*

Love in action is the answer to every
problem in our lives and in this world.
Love in action is the force that helped
us make it to this place, and it's the
truth that will set us free.

Susan Taylor

Gwendolyn Brooks

I was happy to have children . . . I
wanted my body, as well as my mind
and spirit, to succeed, to reach an
appropriate glory.

Love stretches your heart and makes
you big inside.

Margaret Walker

I want to die while you love me,
    While yet you hold me fair,
While laughter lies upon my lips
    And lights are in my hair.

I want to die while you love me,
    And bear to that still bed,
Your kisses turbulent, unspent,
    To warm me when I'm dead.

I want to die while you love me,
    Oh, who would care to live
Till love has nothing more to ask
    And nothing more to give!

I want to die while you love me
    And never never see
The glory of this perfect day
    Grow dim or cease to be.

Georgia Douglas Johnson

I heard that paper read yesterday, that
says 'all men are born equal, and that
every man has a right to freedom . . .'
won't the law give me my freedom?

Elizabeth "Mumbett" Freeman

No man may make another free.

Zora Neale Hurston

Echoes of Harlem *Faith Ringgold*

20 x 20", pastel and collage. 1994. Courtesy of the artist.

The greatest gift is not being
afraid to question.

Ruby Dee

In every human Breast, God has
implanted a principle which we call
Love of Freedom; it is impatient of
Oppression and pants for Deliverance.

Phillis Wheatley

Someday the sun is going to shine
down on me in some faraway place.

Mahalia Jackson

When I found I had crossed that line,
I looked at my hands to see if I was the
same person. There was such a glory
over everything; the sun came like gold
through the trees, and over the fields,
and I felt like I was in Heaven.

Harriet Tubman

Dancing *Elizabeth Catlett*

18 x 24", color lithograph. 1990. Collection of Claude A. Lewis, Culver City, California.

The Artist as Dancer Dancing for Her Life *Margo Humphrey*

22 x 30", color lithograph. 1989. Collection of Murphy Rabb Associates, Chicago, Illinois.

Too many of us are hung up on what
we don't have, can't have, or won't ever
have. We spend too much energy
being down, when we could use that
same energy—if not less of it—
doing, or at least trying to do, some
of the things we really want to do.

Terry McMillan

Most people think I am a dreamer.
. . . We need visions for larger things,
for the unfolding and reviewing of
worthwhile things.

Mary McLeod Bethune

When the Negro learns what manner
of man he is spiritually, he will wake
up all over. . . . He will rise in the
majesty of his own soul. He will
glorify the beauty of his own brown
skin . . . and he will redeem his body
and rescue his soul. . . .

Nannie Helen Burroughs

Movin' On *Irmagean*

30 x 40", charcoal. Copyright © Irmagean, 1979. Collection of Atty. W. Wilson, Oakland, California.

The principal horror of any system which defines the good in terms of profit rather than in terms of human need to the exclusion of the psychic and emotional components of that need—the principal horror of such a system is that it robs our work of its erotic value, its erotic power and life appeal and fulfillment. Such a system reduces work to a travesty of necessities, a duty by which we earn bread or oblivion for ourselves and those we love. But this is tantamount to blinding a painter and then telling her to improve her work and enjoy the art of painting. It is not only next to impossible, it is also profoundly cruel.

The Lord puts pictures in my head,
and he means me to paint them.

Clementine Hunter

The artist . . . is the voice of the people.

Alice Walker

Autobiography: "Who do You Think You Are? One of Us!" *Howardena Pindell*

71.5" diameter, mixed media on sewn canvas. Copyright © Howardena Pindell, 1991-2. Courtesy of the artist.

. . . human beings cannot be willed
and molded into nonexistence.

Angela Davis

Neither character nor standing
avails the Negro if he dares to
protect himself against the white
man or become his rival.

Ida B. Wells

I had to make my own living and my
own opportunity . . . . Don't sit down
and wait for the opportunities to come;
you have to get up and make them.

Madame C. J. Walker

Never, never let a person know you're frightened.

Maya Angelou

3rd and Western *Phoebe Beasley*

36 x 36", collage. 1981. Collection of Terry D'Angona, Los Angeles, California.

Earl's Hair Odyssey *Marie Johnson Calloway*

96 x 80", mixed media. 1985. Courtesy of the artist.

It's easy to be independent when
you've got money. But to be
independent when you haven't got
a thing—that's the Lord's test.

Mahalia Jackson

Where there is money, there is fighting.

Marian Anderson

Money is the sun that makes you shine.

June Jordan

. . . while the continuously gorgeous
panorama of Harlem fascinated her,
thrilled her, the sober, mad rush of
white New York failed entirely to
stir her . . . Of that white world, so
distant, so near, she asked only
indifference. No, not at all from
those pale and powerful people did
she crave awareness. Sinister folk,
she considered them . . .

Nella Larsen

74 x 69", acrylic on canvas with pieced borders. Copyright © Faith Ringgold Inc., 1988.
Collection of the Solomon R. Guggenheim Museum, New York, New York.

The greatest gift I've ever had was
the birth of my son . . . because
of him, I educated myself . . .
I started my lifelong love affair
with libraries . . . I've learned an
awful lot because of him.

Maya Angelou

Lorraine Hansberry

[God] did give us children to make
[our] dreams seem worthwhile.

28 x 20", prismacolor drawing. 1993. Collection of Demetri Cameron, Los Angeles, California.

31 x 23", watercolor. 1989. Courtesy of the artist.

Don't let anything stop you.
There will be times when you'll be
disappointed, but you can't stop.
Make yourself the very best that
you can make out of what you are.
The very best.

Sadie Tanner Mossell Alexander

While it's great to be black and
beautiful . . . it's even better to be
black and beautiful and prepared.

Martina Arroyo

I think long and hard about what my novels should do. They should clarify the roles that have become obscured, they ought to identify those things in the past that are useful and those that are not and they ought to give nourishment.

Toni Morrison

It is the mind that makes the body.

Sojourner Truth

You can kill a man, but you can't kill an idea.

Myrlie Beasley Evers Williams

45 x 28", color lithograph. 1990. Collection of Marshall Erdman & Associates, Madison, Wisconsin.

He, that Great Spirit, who created all
men free and equal . . . He will shake
the tree of liberty, and its blossoms
shall spread all over the earth.

Sarah Forten

Zora Neale Hurston
No matter how far a person can go
the horizon is still way beyond you.

[Pride] . . . If you haven't got it,
you can't show it. If you have got it,
you can't hide it.

Zora Neale Hurston

[Langston Hughes] believed in the
beauty of blackness when belief in the
beauty of blackness was not the
fashion, not "the thing," not the sweet
berry of the community tooth.

Gwendolyn Brooks

Zora and Langston   *Phoebe Beasley*

36 x 36", collage. 1988. Collection of Ron and Charlayne Hunter-Gault, New York, New York.

Sharecropper *Elizabeth Catlett*

18 x 16.5", color linocut. 1968. Collection of Mr. & Mrs. Mack D. Anderson, Claremont, California.

That man over there says that women
need to be helped into carriages, and
lifted over ditches, and to have the
best place everywhere. Nobody ever
helps me into carriages, over mud
puddles, or gives me any best place!
And ain't I a woman? . . . I have
plowed and planted and gathered into
barns, and no man could head me—
and ain't I a woman? I could work as
much and eat as much as a man
(when I could get it), and bear the
lash as well—and ain't I a woman?
I have borne thirteen children and
seen them most all sold off into
slavery, and when I cried out with a
mother's grief, none but Jesus heard—
and ain't I a woman?

Anything that is as old as racism is in the blood line of the nation. It's not any superficial thing—that attitude is in the blood and we have to educate it out.

Nannie Helen Burroughs

America is not a safe place.

Ntozake Shange

Autobiography: Water/Ancestors/
Middle Passage/Family Ghosts *Howardena Pindell*

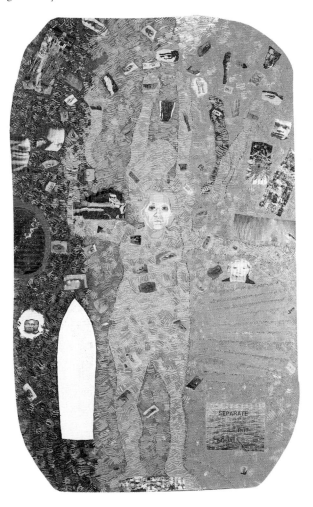

118 x 71", mixed media on sewn canvas. Copyright © Howardena Pindell, 1988. Courtesy of the Wadsworth
Atheneum, Hartford, Connecticut; Ella Gallup Sumner and Mary Catlin Sumner Collection.

Ties that Bind *Irmagean*

23.5 x 35.25", charcoal. 1980. On loan to Departmento de Bellas Artes, Guadalajara, Mexico.

They sang to forget the chains
and misery. The sorrow will one
day turn to joy. All that breaks the
heart and oppresses the soul will
one day give place to peace and
understanding, and every man will
be free. That is the interpretation
of a true Negro spiritual.

Susan Robeson

Find the Good and Praise It   *Phoebe Beasley*

24 x 36", collage. 1994. Collection of Abe and Launa Thompson, Chicago, Illinois.

The human race does command its
own destiny and that destiny can
eventually embrace the stars.

Lorraine Hansberry

I know one race—the human race.

Osceola Macarthy Archer Adams

There comes a point when you really
have to spend time with yourself to
know who you are. Black people need
to be with ourselves.

Bernice Johnson Reagon

Ma Rainey

White folks hear the blues come out,
but they don't know how it got there.

Hope Street   *Marie Johnson Calloway*

96 x 68", mixed media. 1971–85. Collection of the Port of Oakland, Oakland, California.

Until we have the right to speak out
and raise our voices in protest, then
no one of us will be free.   *Eleanor Holmes Norton*

We must trust the people. We must
trust each other . . . We must protect
our own basic rights by protecting
the rights of others.

Faye Wattleton

Talk without effort is nothing.

Maria W. Stewart

Nikki Giovanni

His headstone said
Free at last, Free at last
But death is a slave's freedom
We seek the freedom of free men
And the construction of a world
Where Martin Luther King
        could have lived
    and preached nonviolence.

I'm sick and tired of being sick and tired.

Fannie Lou Hamer

I would fight for my liberty so long as
my strength lasted, and if the time
came for me to go, the Lord would let
them take me.

Harriet Tubman

The History of Her Life Written Across Her Face   *Margo Humphrey*

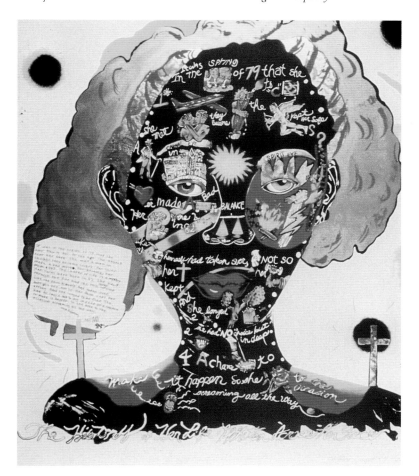

45 x 45", color lithograph with gold foil and chine collé. 1992. Collection of the Museum of Modern Art, New York, New York.

Untitled *Edythe Boone*

20 x 18", pastel and collage. 1993. Courtesy of the artist.

Let us labor to acquire knowledge, to
break down the barriers of prejudice
and oppression believing, that if not
for us, for another generation, there is
a brighter day in store.

Charlotte Forten

Education is the jewel casting
brilliance into the future.

Mari Evans

Groovin' High   *Faith Ringgold*

Life is a marvelous,
transitory adventure.

Nikki Giovanni

We are the only racial group within
the United States ever forbidden by
law to read and write.

Alice Childress

Everyone else is represented in
Washington by a rich and powerful
lobby, it seems. But there is no lobby
for the people.

Shirley Chisholm

It's a tremendous responsibility—a responsibility and an honor—to be a cultural worker . . . whatever you call this vocation. One's got to see what the welfare children see, what the scholar sees, got to see what the ruling class mythmakers see as well, in order to tell the truth and not get trapped.

Toni Cade Bambara

We never lost hope despite the
segregated world of this rural town
because we had adults who gave us a
sense of a future—and black folk had
an extra lot of problems, and we were
taught that we could struggle and
change them.

Marian Wright Edelman

We didn't have any of what they
called Civil Rights back then. It was
just a matter of survival—existing
from day to day.

Rosa Parks

Circa 1943 *Phoebe Beasley*

36 x 36", collage. 1983. Collection of Camille Love, Atlanta, Georgia.

Hardworking Father *Edythe Boone*

35.5 x 17", oil. 1983. Courtesy of the artist.

When you love a man, he becomes
more than a body. His physical
limbs expand, and his outline
recedes, vanishes. He is rich and
sweet and right. He is part of the
world, the atmosphere, the blue sky
and the blue water.

Gwendolyn Brooks

When do any of us do enough?

Barbara Jordan

I taught my students . . . that every
person is sacred.

Margaret Walker

There are no people that need all the
benefits resulting from a well-directed
education more than we do. The
condition of our people, the wants of
our children, and the welfare of our
race demand the aid of every helping
hand. It is a work of time, a labor of
patience, to become an effective school
teacher; and it should be a work of
love in which they who engage should
not abate heart or hope.

Frances Ellen Watkins Harper

Royal Sacrifice *Samella Lewis*

36 x 24", oil. 1969. Collection of Hampton University Museum, Hampton, Virginia.

Untitled   *Howardena Pindell*

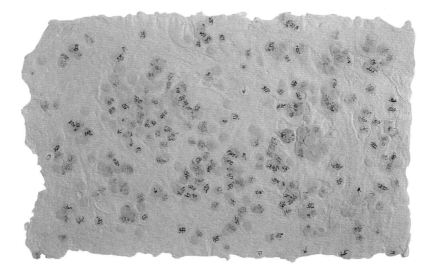

6.25 x 10.5", handmade paper with embedded drawings in pen and ink. Copyright © Howardena Pindell, 1975. Courtesy of the artist.

We, the black women of today,
must accept the full weight of a
legacy wrought in blood by our
mothers in chains. As heirs of a
tradition of perseverance and heroic
resistance, we must hasten to take
our place wherever our people are
forging toward freedom.

Angela Davis

Jamaica Kincaid

I hope never to be at peace. I hope to
make my life manageable, and I think it's
fairly manageable now. But, oh, I would
never accept peace. That means death.

I walked down the street didn't have
     on no hat,
Asking everybody I meet,
Where's my man at.

Ma Rainey

Love rejected hurts so much more than
love rejecting.

Lucille Clifton

The spirit of the marriage left the
bedroom and took to living in the parlor.

You see me ravin', you hear me crying,
Oh Lawd, this lonely heart of mine,
Sometimes, I'm grieving from my hat
    down to my shoes.
I'm a good-hearted woman that's a
    slave to the blues.

Ma Rainey

Homage to Sister Gertrude Morgan   *Margo Humphrey*

12 x 12", black and white lithograph. 1990. Collection of Bank of America, San Francisco, California.

People see God every day. They just
don't recognize him.   *Pearl Bailey*

Can't nothing make your life work if
you ain't the architect.

Terry McMillan

Woman, if the soul of the nation
is to be saved, I believe that you must
become its soul.

Coretta Scott King

The shortness of time, the certainty
of death, and the instability of
all things here induce me to turn my
thoughts from earth to heaven.

Maria W. Stewart

Church Mothers *Marie Johnson Calloway*

48 x 90", mixed media. 1986. Collection of California Afro-American Museum, Los Angeles, California.

I am a black woman
the music of my song
some sweet arpeggio of tears
is written in a minor key
and I
can be heard humming in the night
Can be heard
                humming
in the night

Mari Evans

Dancing on the George Washington Bridge *Faith Ringgold*

Osceola Macarthy Archer Adams (1890–1983) After obtaining a graduate degree in drama from New York University, Adams went on to an illustrious stage career, co-starring in numerous modern classics such as *The Emperor Jones* (opposite Paul Robeson) and *Panic* (with Orson Welles).

Sadie Tanner Mossell Alexander (1898–1989) Born into a prominent Philadelphia family, she was the first African-American woman in the United States to earn a Ph.D. in economics (University of Pennsylvania, June 6, 1921). Following that achievement, she went on to earn a law degree with honors from the University of Pennsylvania in 1927. In partnership with her husband, Harvard-educated lawyer Raymond Pace Alexander, she was one of the founders of the National Bar Association, the professional organization for African-American lawyers. Dr. Alexander and her husband were renowned crusaders for civil rights from the 1920s through the 1940s in the Philadelphia area.

Marian Anderson (1902–1994) The first African-American to sing at the Metropolitan Opera, Anderson was praised by the great conductor Arturo Toscanini as having a voice "heard only once in a lifetime." One of the most famous events of her life occurred on Easter mórning, 1943, when Anderson gave a concert for 75,000 people on the steps of the Lincoln Memorial at the invitation of Eleanor Roosevelt.

Maya Angelou (1928–) Best known for the first volume of her autobiography, *I Know Why the Caged Bird Sings*, Angelou has enjoyed a rich career as a performer, writer, and director. She is a prolific writer of prose, poetry, and theatrical and television plays.

Martina Arroyo (1937–) Although she began her career as a teacher and caseworker with the New York City Welfare Department, world-renowned opera star Arroyo never lost sight of her dream for a life in the arts. She made her debut in 1958 at Carnegie Hall, and a year later she sang at the Metropolitan Opera, where she was a mainstay for ten years. She is highly regarded as an interpreter of Verdi's operas.

Pearl Bailey (1918–1990) Actress, singer, comedienne, and special envoy to the United Nations, the versatile Bailey began her career singing with Count Basie's Orchestra. She went on to create memorable characters in movies such as *Carmen Jones* and *Porgy and Bess*, and won a Tony Award for her starring role in the stage production of *Hello, Dolly*.

Ella Baker (1903–1986) One of the towering, often unsung, heroines of black political activism, Baker was a crucial force in shaping African-American, twentieth-century radical philosophy. From her cooperative campaign work in Harlem during the Depression through her involvement with the WPA, to her field work for the NAACP and her founding of the Student Non-violent Coordinating Committee (SNCC), Baker always strove for democratized, grass-roots, decentralized leadership. Her life is documented in the film *Fundi*.

Josephine Baker (1906–1975) Like so many black entertainers, Baker got her start in the musical *Shuffle Along*, and later toured with blues legend Bessie Smith. Her greatest fame, however, came with her move to Paris in *La Revue Negre* after which she enjoyed sensational popularity and critical adulation for decades. She was also admired for her humanitarian efforts on behalf of orphans of mixed-race backgrounds.

Toni Cade Bambara (1939–   ) Her first book, *Gorilla, My Love*, written in 1972, was a short story collection that focused on the lives of young girls. Her 1981 novel, *The Salt Eaters*, won the American Book Award for fiction. In addition to her writing, Bambara has taught English and African Studies and is a noted civil rights activist.

Mary McLeod Bethune (1875–1955) Educator, civil rights leader, presidential advisor, and government official, Bethune decided at the age of twenty to devote her life to the education of black people. She was a member of the National Child Welfare Commission under Presidents Coolidge and Hoover, and was Director of the Division of Minority Affairs under Franklin Delano Roosevelt.

Gwendolyn Brooks (1917–   ) In 1950, Gwendolyn Brooks became the first African-American to win the Pulitzer Prize, for her second book of poetry, *Annie Allen*. Brooks is an acclaimed member of the literary establishment which has elected her as member of the National Academy of Arts and Letters and selected her as the first African-American poetry consultant to the Library of Congress.

Nannie Helen Burroughs (1879–1961) Orator, religious leader, political organizer, civil rights leader, and educator, Burroughs achieved national prominence by founding the Women's Convention Auxiliary at the National Baptist Convention. For sixty years she led the WCA in the struggle for women's rights, antilynching laws, desegregation, and industrial education for black women and girls.

Alice Childress (1920–1994) Playwright, novelist, actress, and director, Childress is best known for her play *Wedding Band: A Love/Hate Story in Black and White.* Her screen adaptation of her young adult novel, *A Hero Ain't Nothin' but a Sandwich,* won the first Paul Robeson Award for outstanding contributions to the performing arts from the Black Filmmakers Hall of Fame.

Shirley Chisholm (1924–) A longtime civil rights activist and educator, Chisholm was the first black woman elected to Congress, in 1969. Her autobiography, *Unbought and Unbossed,* reflects the determination and integrity that have been the personal and professional hallmarks of her life.

Lucille Clifton (1936–) Clifton's first book of poetry, *Good Times,* was named by *The New York Times* as one of the ten best books of the year when it was published in 1969. She has also been the recipient of several National Endowment for the Arts grants, and her poetry collection *Two Headed Woman* was nominated for a Pulitzer Prize.

Bessie Coleman (1896–1926) Because of racism in the United States, Coleman emigrated to France to receive schooling in the fledgling field of aviation. Returning to America as a certified aviator, barnstormer, and parachutist, she performed primarily for African-American audiences until her untimely death at the age of thirty.

Angela Yvonne Davis (1944–) Writer, educator, and activist, Davis is a nationally known political theorist who has twice run for vice president on the Communist Party ticket.

She studied philosophy at the University of California with Herbert Marcuse, who considered her the best student he had ever taught. Her essays are collected in *Women, Race, and Class* and *Women, Culture, and Politics.*

Ruby Dee (1923–) One of the most talented and versatile actresses of our time, Dee is also a noted activist, director, and writer whose works include *Glowchild and Other Poems* and *Two Ways to Count to Ten.* She has performed on stage and screen, often with her husband, Ossie Davis.

Marian Wright Edelman (1939–) Civil rights activist, author, and children's advocate, Edelman attended Yale University Law School, later headed the Harvard University Center for Law and Education, and founded the Children's Defense Fund. She is the first African-American woman elected to the Yale University Corporation, is a MacArthur Foundation fellow, and the recipient of more than thirty honorary degrees.

Mari Evans (1923–) A versatile and widely published author of stories, poems, plays, and musicals, Evans won the Indiana University Writers' Conference Award and the Black Academy of Arts and Letters Award for her poetry collection, *I Am a Black Woman.*

Jessie Redmon Fauset (c. 1885–1961) A prominent novelist of the Harlem Renaissance, Fauset wrote about black women of her time, and received acclaim for her portraits of middle- and upper-class black families. For several years, she was the literary editor of *The Crisis,* the magazine of the NAACP, a position from which she influenced a wide circle of young writers, including poet Langston Hughes.

Charlotte Forten (1837–1914) The granddaughter of noted abolitionist James Forten, Charlotte Forten wrote poetry and was a teacher for many years. She was an active abolitinist before the Civil War, and worked to help freed slaves in South Carolina after the war. Her enduring distinction, however, derives from her detailed diary, which offers intimate insights into the lives of black people before and during the Civil War. At 41, she married Francis James Grimke.

Sarah Forten (1814–1883) The aunt of abolitionist Charlotte Forten Grimke, Sarah Forten began publishing her antislavery writing in *The Liberator* at the age of seventeen. She was a charter member of the Philadelphia Female Anti-Slavery Society, and though she married Joseph Purvis in 1838 to pursue a career as a wife and mother, she never abandoned her lifetime crusade for the emancipation of slaves.

Elizabeth "Mumbett" Freeman (c. 1742–1829) The plaintiff in an historic civil rights suit, Freeman had been enslaved by Col. John Ashley, but left his house after a brutal assault. While waiting tables, she overheard conversations about the Bill of Rights and the new Constitution of Massachusetts. A prominent young attorney, Theodore Sedgewick, argued against Freeman's enslavement by Ashley and won the case in county court, thereby establishing the illegality of slavery in Massachusetts.

Nikki Giovanni (1943–   ) In addition to publishing more than ten books of poetry and prose, Giovanni is a widely anthologized poet, who first won fame in the sixties when her writing dramatized the development of a young black woman into a militant activist. She won a National Book Award nomination for her collection *Gemini* and continues to write and lecture. A TV film about her life, *Spirit to Spirit: The Poetry of Nikki Giovanni*, has been broadcast on public television.

Fannie Lou Hamer (1917–1977) Sharecropper and activist, Miz Hamer, as she was widely known, endured beatings and imprisonment in her struggle for voter registration. She was a field secretary for the Student Nonviolent Coordinating Committee (SNCC) and a founder of the Mississippi Freedom Democratic Party. Her life is chronicled in the biography *This Little Light of Mine.*

Lorraine Hansberry (1930–1965) Best known for her award-winning play *A Raisin in the Sun*, Hansberry was the first African-American woman to have a play produced on Broadway. Her husband compiled and edited Hansberry's autobiographical writing into the work *To Be Young, Gifted, and Black*, which itself became a play. Hansberry's last play, *Les Blancs*, was produced after her death at the age of thirty-four.

Frances Ellen Watkins Harper (1825–1911) A prolific writer of prose and poetry, Harper was also an active member of the Underground Railroad and a founder of the American Women's Suffrage Association and the National Association of Colored Women. Her best-known novel is *Iola Leroy*, published in 1892.

Clementine Hunter (1886–1988) A prominent folk artist, Hunter did not begin her career until the age of fifty-three, but she is believed to have completed more than five thousand paintings prized for their vivid colors and whimsical humor.

Zora Neale Hurston (c. 1901–1960) One of the major writers of the Harlem Renaissance, Hurston has inspired many other black writers, including Alice Walker. She studied anthropology with Franz Boas on a scholarship at Barnard College, and with the aid of a Rosenwald Fellowship and two Guggenheim Fellowships, she traveled to the Caribbean and the South to study black folklore. A prolific writer of novels, short stories, plays, essays, and scholarly articles, Hurston is best known for her novel *Their Eyes Were Watching God.*

Mahalia Jackson (1911–1972) One of the greatest gospel singers of all time, Jackson began singing in storefront churches where she caught the attention of Professor Thomas A. Dorsey, the "Father of Gospel Music," who became her mentor. Jackson's recording of "Move On Up a Little Higher" sold more than eight million copies in 1947 and made her an international star. She combined her commercial success in the movies, TV, and radio with commitment to African-American causes through her tireless and open support of Dr. Martin Luther King. Jackson sang at the 1963 March on Washington.

Georgia Douglas Johnson (1886–1966) Poet, playwright, and journalist, Johnson was one of the most important figures of the Harlem Renaissance, and her home was a literary salon for over forty years. She graduated from Oberlin College and was one of the first African-American women to achieve national recognition as a poet. Her books include *The Heart of a Woman, Bronze,* and *Autumn Love Cycle.*

Barbara Jordan (1936–   ) The first black woman from a southern state to serve in Congress, Jordan achieved national recognition during the Watergate hearings. In 1976, she became the first black keynote speaker at the Democratic National Convention; she again addressed the convention in 1992. Jordan holds twenty-nine honorary degrees and is a professor of government at the University of Texas.

June Jordan (1936–   ) The author of nineteen books of prose and poetry, Jordan has served on the faculties of Yale University, Connecticut College, and City College of New York. She is currently a professor of African-American Studies and Women's Studies at the University of California, Berkeley. Jordan has won a Rockefeller grant as well as a fellowship in poetry from the National Endowment for the Humanities.

Florence Griffith Joyner (1959–   ) Born in Los Angeles, Joyner began running track at the age of seven, and at fourteen and fifteen she won the Jesse Owens National Youth Games Award. Now a world famous track star and Olympic gold medalist, Joyner holds seven world records.

Jamaica Kincaid (1949–   ) Born Elaine Potter Richardson in St. Johns, Antigua, Kincaid left the Caribbean at age sixteen to pursue a writing career in New York. After contributing incisive and witty pieces on a regular basis to *The New Yorker*, Kincaid became a staff writer at the magazine in 1976. She has since written many acclaimed novels and short stories.

Coretta Scott King (1927–   ) An accomplished musician and singer, Coretta Scott King earned a B.A. in music from Antioch College and then enrolled for further study at the New England Conservatory of Music. She met Dr. Martin Luther King in Boston and later married him. After his assassination in 1968, she became the founding president of the Martin Luther King Jr. Center for Nonviolent Social Change in Atlanta.

Nella Larsen (1893–1963) One of the few women writers of the Harlem Renaissance, Larsen is the author of *Quicksand* and *Passing*, which both deal with interracial heritage and the search for a black culture and identity. In 1930, Larsen became the first black woman to receive a Guggenheim Fellowship, which gave her the financial freedom to write. She published no more, however, and little is known of her later years, other than that she returned to her career as a nurse.

Audre Lorde (1934–1992) Refusing to be categorized in her personal or professional life, Lorde was a poet, novelist, wife, mother, lesbian activist, and finally, cancer victim. One of her most widely acclaimed works is the poetry collection *Black Unicorn.*

Terry McMillan (1951–) After graduating from the University of California, Berkeley, with a B.A. in journalism, McMillan went on to earn an M.A. in film from Columbia University. She began her first novel, *Mama,* while a fellow at the MacDowell Colony and marketed it herself, eventually making it into a best-seller. Her following books, *Disappearing Acts* and *Waiting to Exhale,* were also best-sellers. She has also edited an anthology of black writing called *Breaking Ice.*

Toni Morrison (1931–) A Nobel and Pulitzer Prize–winning author, Morrison has achieved the pinnacle of success in her field. Born Chloe Anthony Wofford, Morrison grew up in a home steeped in African-American myth, folklore, language and songs, all of which form a context for her writing. Her first novel, *The Bluest Eye,* is still a favorite among her readers, while *The Song of Solomon* won the American Book Critics Circle Award. *Beloved,* the tragic and deeply moving novel of infanticide, won the Pulitzer Prize. In 1993, she became the first African-American woman to win the Nobel Prize for Literature. She has been on the faculties of Yale, Princeton, the State University of New York, and Bard College, among others.

Eleanor Holmes Norton (1937–) Born in Washington, D.C., Norton graduated from Dunbar High School as a member of its last segregated class. She earned a B.A. from Antioch College, and M.A. and J.D. degrees from Yale University. After working for the Mississippi Freedom Democratic Party, Norton went on to a position with the ACLU (American Civil Liberties Union), where she specialized in First Amendment cases. The recipient of more than fifty honorary degrees, Norton was the first woman to chair the Equal Employment Opportunities Commission, under President Carter.

Rosa Parks (1913–) Seamstress Rosa Parks began the modern civil rights movement when she refused to surrender her seat to a white man on a crowded bus in Montgomery, Alabama. This sparked the Montgomery bus boycotts, which brought Dr. Martin Luther King to prominence and led to the desegregation of public transportation in Montgomery.

Ma Rainey (1886–1939) Born Gertrude Pridgett, Ma Rainey, known as the "Mother of the Blues," popularized the blues—a sound that combined the black rural traditions of spirituals and work songs with the raw rhythms of honky-tonks and bars. Rainey traveled the vaudeville circuit, often performing with minstrel shows, but in spite of making ninety successful recordings, Rainey's singing career waned. She retired to manage two theaters she owned in Rome, Georgia.

Bernice Johnson Reagon (1942–) A civil rights activist as a student, Reagon is a founding member of the singing group Sweet Honey in the Rock. Reagon has received a MacArthur Foundation fellowship and is also a curator at the Smithsonian Institution.

Susan Robeson (1953–) The granddaughter of Eslanda and Paul Robeson, Susan Robeson is an editor and TV producer who has published a collection of her grandfather's writings, *He's Got the Whole World in His Hands.*

Wilma Rudolph (1940–1994) Born into a poor, rural family with twenty-two children, Rudolph had to overcome bouts of polio and scarlet fever that left her virtually crippled at the age of four. She went on to win three gold medals in track at the Rome Olympics in 1960.

Ntozake Shange (1948–) Born Paulette Williams in Trenton, New Jersey, Shange assumed the Zulu names "she who comes with her own things" and "she who walks like a lion" as an act of protest against her Western roots. She has a B.A. from Barnard College and an M.A. from the University of California, Berkeley. A prolific poet and playwright, Shange won an Obie Award for her "choreopoem" *for colored girls who have considered suicide / when the rainbow is enuf.*

Maria W. Stewart (1803–1879) Orator and writer, Stewart was the first American-born woman to engage in public political dialogue when she began her brief speaking career in 1836. She advocated black self-determination and economic independence.

Susan Taylor (1946–) As the editor of *Essence* magazine, Taylor has exercised influence over a whole generation of contemporary black readers.

Sojourner Truth (c. 1797–1883) Born in New York and originally named Isabella (Belle) Bomefree, she was one of the great abolitionist speakers of her time. After a profound religious experience in 1843, she changed her name and continued her stirring speeches at camp meetings, churches, and conventions. Renowned for her support of righteous causes, Sojourner Truth's name and life have inspired generations of African-Americans.

Harriet Tubman (c. 1821–1913) The Moses of her people, Tubman helped some three hundred African-Americans come north to freedom after she herself escaped slavery at the age of twenty-five. She was an active abolitionist, a supporter of John Brown's revolt, and, during the Civil War, a scout and spy for the Union.

Alice Walker (1944–) Novelist, poet, essayist, and activist, Walker was born in Eatonton, Georgia, and was educated at Sarah Lawrence College, where she began writing fiction. Her novel *The Color Purple* brought her critical and popular acclaim, winning a Pulitzer Prize, an American Book Award, and a National Book Critics Circle Award nomination. She has published more than fifteen volumes of prose and poetry that reflect a rich tapestry of African and African-American life. Walker is credited with reviving public interest in the work of Harlem Renaissance writer Zora Neale Hurston.

Madame C. J. Walker (1867–1919) One of America's first black millionaires, C. J. Walker rose from rags to riches through her invention of African-American beauty products and her innovative, prescient marketing techniques.

Margaret Walker (1915–) Her award-winning novel *Jubilee* was one of the first modern novels to recount slavery from the slaves' point of view. Walker graduated from Northwestern University and holds a Ph.D. in English from the University of Iowa.

She has won many awards and grants for her prose and poetry including a Houghton-Mifflin Literary Fellowship, a Ford Foundation Fellowship, a National Endowment for the Arts grant, and a Fulbright. Her other works include *For My People* and *Ballad of the Free*.

Faye Wattleton (1943–   ) Born in St. Louis, Wattleton was the first person in her family to earn a college degree, and she went on to earn an M.S. in maternal and infant care. When she was appointed Executive Director of the Planned Parenthood Association of America in 1978, Wattleton was the first woman, first African-American, and the youngest person to head the organization. She retired from that position in 1991.

Ida B. Wells (1862–1931) Journalist, lecturer, civil rights leader, and antilynching campaigner, Wells was one of the founding members of the NAACP. *The Red Record*, her major antilynching work, was published in 1895. She also founded the first black women's suffrage organization.

Phillis Wheatley (c. 1753–1784) Although she grew up a slave, Wheatley won widespread fame as a poet. At a time when many white people in America considered Africans and African-Americans to be almost less than human, Wheatley's literary accomplishments challenged these cruel stereotypes. She was the second woman (after Anne Bradstreet) and first black to publish a book of poetry, in 1773. Her work was celebrated in both the United States and England, and continues to be studied today.

Fannie Barrier Williams (1855–1944) Although she grew up in an affluent, integrated community in Brockport, New York, Williams learned the harsh realities of racism when she went south to teach during the 1870s. The experience politicized her and she built a reputation as a reformer devoted to social change, feminism, and the education of African-Americans.

Myrlie Beasley Evers Williams (c. 1932–   ) The widow of slain civil rights leader Medgar Evers, Myrlie Evers Williams shared his commitment to the cause, and has kept his reputation and sacrifice before the public primarily through her book *For Us the Living*. Still an activist, Williams currently serves as president of the NAACP.

Oprah Winfrey (1954–   ) In spite of being born in rural poverty and suffering sexual abuse, Winfrey has become a media phenomenon. She has achieved international influence, celebrity, and wealth as a TV star, actress, producer, and communications entrepreneur.

Phoebe Beasley (1943–) Beasley has had several one-woman exhibitions, both in the United States and abroad. In 1989 she was commissioned to do the artwork and official poster for the Presidential Inauguration, and she is the only artist to twice receive the Presidential Seal. Her work is included in the private collections of Oprah Winfrey, Maya Angelou, and Magic Johnson.

Edythe Boone (1938–) A committed artist and activist, Boone has helped to create many of the murals that illuminate the buildings and walls of the Bay Area, including the celebrated collaborative mural covering San Francisco's Women's Building. She lives and works in Richmond, California, where she teaches painting, drawing, and crafts to children at the Richmond Art Center.

Marie Johnson Calloway (1920–) Calloway has shown her work in numerous venues, including the Oakland Museum, Howard University, and the Brockman Gallery in Los Angeles. She has been an art professor at several Bay Area schools, and she continues to exhibit, take on public commissions, and lecture widely. Her unique installations bear the influence of the Depression, the Harlem Renaissance, and the political struggles of the 1960s.

Elizabeth Catlett (1919–) Known internationally as a printmaker and a sculptor, Catlett's work focuses primarily on women. Her works are featured in the Museum of Modern Art in New York and the New Orleans Museum of Art, as well as many prominent private collections. Catlett, who lectures frequently on human rights, is an outspoken critic of the status of African-Americans and Mexicans in the U.S.

Margo Humphrey (1942–) In addition to being an accomplished printmaker, Humphrey has written and illustrated a children's book, *The River That Gave Gifts*. Her works are included in the permanent collections of the Museum of Modern Art in New York and the Smithsonian Institute in Washington, D.C., among others. Having taught in many parts of the world, including Fiji, Humphrey now lives in Maryland and teaches at the University of Maryland in College Park.

Irmagean (1947–) Since receiving a BFA from California College of Arts and Crafts in 1976, Irmagean has exhibited internationally in Czechoslovakia and Germany, as well as numerous Bay Area venues, and has won several awards. She uses the imagery of dancers to illustrate the interplay of the individual and the group, emphasizing curve and movement.

Samella Lewis (1924–) Artist, educator, curator, and collector, Lewis creates works ranging from painting and sculpture to printmaking, several of which are included in the collections of the Oakland Museum, The High Museum (in Atlanta), and the Virginia Museum of Fine Art. Lewis, who is also known for her films on African-American artists, lives and works in Los Angeles.

Howardena Pindell (1943–) Having received her BFA from Boston University and her MFA from Yale University's School of Art and Architecture, Pindell has gone on to earn numerous awards and fellowships, including a Guggenheim Award for painting and a fellowship in Japan. In 1996 she will receive an award from the Women's Caucus for distinguished contribution to the art profession. Ms. Pindell is currently a professor of art at SUNY Stonybrook.

Faith Ringgold (1930–) Mixed-media sculptor, performance artist, writer, and teacher, Ringgold is primarily known for her intricate, African-inspired storytelling quilts. She has also written and illustrated several distinguished children's books and has won countless awards and honors. She is currently a professor of art at the University of California at San Diego.

PERMISSIONS

Every effort has been made to track down permissions for the works included in this book. If something has been overlooked, please alert the publisher. We gratefully acknowledge the following for allowing their works to be excerpted for this book.

Mari Evans: "I Am a Black Woman" from *I Am a Black Woman* by Mari Evans. Published by William Morrow & Co. Inc., New York, 1970; reprinted by permission of Mari Evans Phemster, copyright © 1970 by Mari Evans.

Nikki Giovanni: "Free at Last" from *Black Feeling Black Talk/Judgement* by Nikki Giovanni. Reprinted by permission of William Morrow & Co. Inc., New York, 1970. Copyright ©1970 by Nikki Giovanni.

Georgia Douglas Johnson: "I Want to Die While You Love Me" in *Caroling Dusk*, ed., Countee Cullen. Published by Harper & Brothers, New York, 1927.

SOURCES

p. 3. Mary McLeod Bethune. "Last Will and Testament." *Ebony* magazine, August 1955 (reprinted September 1963, November 1973).

p. 5. Susan Taylor. *In the Spirit: The Inspirational Writings of Susan Taylor.* New York: Essence Communications, 1985. Sojourner Truth. *The Narrative of Sojourner Truth, A Northern Slave Emancipated from Bodily Slavery by the State of New York in 1828*, written down by Olive Gilbert. Boston: 1850.

p. 6. Oprah Winfrey. "An Intimate Talk With Oprah." *Essence* magazine, August 1987. Josephine Baker. "Black Venus Returns," by Garrett Ward. *The New York Times*, May 19, 1951.

p. 9. Ella Baker. *Fundi: The Story of Ella Baker.* TV documentary by Joanne Grant, 1981. Wilma Rudolph. From a private conversation with Elizabeth Ryan. May 1974.

p. 10. Sarah Forten. From a poem commissioned for the Convention of American Women, 1837; reprinted in *Black Women in America*, eds. Darlene Clark Hine, Elsa Barkley Brown, Rosalyn Terborg Penn. Bloomington: Indiana University Press, 1993. Jesse Redmon Fauset. *Plum Bun: A Novel Without a Moral.* New York: Frederick A. Stokes, 1928.

p. 13. Maria W. Stewart. *Maria Stewart: America's First Woman Political Writer*, ed. Marilyn Richardson. Bloomington: Indiana University Press, 1987.

p. 14. Harriet Tubman. *Harriet Tubman: The Moses of Her People*, by Sarah Bradford. New York: J. Little & Co., 1886. Florence Griffith Joyner. "Spotlight: Life in the Fast Lane." *Essence* magazine, March 1989.

p. 15. Bessie Coleman. "Bessie Coleman, Aviation Pioneer." Department of Transportation News (no date), from *Black Women in America*, eds. Darlene Clark Hine, et al. Bloomington: Indiana University Press, 1993.

p. 16. Ida B. Wells. *Crusade for Justice: The Autobiography of Ida B. Wells*, ed. Alfreda Duster. Chicago: University of Chicago Press, 1970. Fannie Barrier Williams. "A Northern Negro's Autobiography." *Independent* magazine, July 14, 1904.

p. 19. Harriet Tubman. Id. Maya Angelou. *Conversations with Maya Angelou*, ed. Jeffrey M. Elliot. New York: Virago, 1988.

p. 20. Mary McLeod Bethune. "Faith That Moved a Dump Heap." *Who, The Magazine About People*, June 1941. Mari Evans. "My Father's Passage," from *I Am a Black Woman*. New York: William Morrow & Co., 1970.

p. 23. June Jordan. *Home Girls: A Black Feminist Anthology*, ed. Barbara Smith. New York: Kitchen Table: Women of Color Press, 1983. Susan Taylor. Id.

p. 24. Gwendolyn Brooks. *Maud Martha: An Autobiographical Novel*. New York: AMS Press, 1974. Margaret Walker. *Jubilee*. Boston: Houghton Mifflin, 1966.

p. 25. Georgia Douglas Johnson. "I Want to Die While You Love Me" in *Caroling Dusk*, ed. Countee Cullen. New York: Harper & Brothers, 1927.

p. 26. Elizabeth "Mumbett" Freeman. From *Brom and Bett v. Ashley*, Massachusetts Court Files, May 1779–October 1783. Zora Neale Hurston. *Moses, Man of the Mountain*. Philadelphia: J.B. Lippincott, 1935.

p. 29. Ruby Dee. *Tower to Heaven*. New York: Third World Press, 1974. Phillis Wheatley. *Memoir and Poems of Phillis Wheatley, A Native African and a Slave*. Boston: George W. Light, 1834.

p. 30. Mahalia Jackson. "I Can't Stop Singing." *The Saturday Evening Post*, December 5, 1959. Harriet Tubman. Id.

p. 33. Terry McMillan. *Mama*. Boston: Houghton Mifflin, 1987. Mary McLeod Bethune. From a speech to the National Council of Negro Women, 1935. Washington, D.C: Bethune Museum Archives, 1981.

p. 34. Nannie Helen Burroughs. "With All They Getting." *The Southern Workman Magazine*, July 1927.

p. 36. Audre Lorde. *A Burst of Light*. Ithaca: Firebrand, 1988.

p. 37. Clementine Hunter. *Clementine Hunter: American Folk Artist*, by James L. Wilson. Los Angeles: Pelican Publishing Co., 1988. Alice Walker. *The Third Life of Grange Copeland*. New York: Harcourt Brace, 1970.

p. 39. Angela Davis. "Lessons from Attica to Soledad." *The New York Times*, October 8, 1971. Ida B. Wells. Id.

p. 40. Madame C. J. Walker. *Textbook of the Madame C. J. Walker Schools of Beauty Culture*, by A'Lelia Walker. New York: Diadem Press, 1928. Maya Angelou. *I Know Why the Caged Bird Sings*. New York: Random House, 1970.

p. 43. Mahalia Jackson. "I Can't Stop Singing."Id. Marian Anderson. *Marian Anderson: A Portrait*, by Kosti Vehanin. Westport, CT: Greenwood Press, 1970; revision of 1940 edition. June Jordan. *Dry Victories*. New York: Henry Holt & Co., 1972.

p. 44. Nella Larsen. *Quicksand*. New York: Alfred A. Knopf, 1928.

p. 46. Maya Angelou. "Maya Angelou: The Heart of the Woman," by Stephanie Stoken Oliver. *Essence* magazine, May 1985. Lorraine Hansberry. *To Be Young, Gifted, and Black: An Informal Autobiography*, adapted by Robert Nemiroff. New York: New American Library, 1970.

p. 49. Sadie Tanner Mossell Alexander. "Sadie Tanner Alexander: At 83, a Woman for Any Age," by Maralyn Lois Polak. *Philadelphia Inquirer Magazine*, March 29, 1981. Martina Arroyo. "Life at the Opera with Madame Butterball," by Alan Levy. *New York Times Magazine*, May 14, 1972.

p. 50. Toni Morrison. *Black Women Writers (1950–1980): A Critical Evaluation*, ed. Mari Evans. Garden City, NY: Anchor/Doubleday, 1984.

p. 51. Sojourner Truth. Id. Myrlie Beasley Evers. *For Us the Living*. Garden City, NY: Doubleday, 1967.

p. 53. Sarah Forten. "The Forten-Purvis Women of Philadelphia and the American Anti-Slavery Crusade," by Janice L. Sumler-Lewis. *Journal of Negro History*, Winter 1981–82. Zora Neale Hurston. *Their Eyes Were Watching God*. Philadelphia: J.B. Lippincott, 1937.

p. 54. Zora Neale Hurston. *Dust Tracks on the Road*. Philadelphia: J.B. Lippincott, 1942. Gwendolyn Brooks. *Report from Part One: The Autobiography of Gwendolyn Brooks*. Detroit: Broadside Press, 1972.

p. 57. Sojourner Truth. Id.

p. 58. Nannie Helen Burroughs. "Unload Your Uncle Toms." *The Louisiana Weekly*, December 23, 1933. Ntozake Shange. "Ntozake Shange Finds the Poetry in Sisterhood." *USA Today*, December 6, 1994.

p. 61. Susan Robeson. *The Whole World in His Hands.* Secaucus, NJ: Citadel Press, 1981.

p. 63. Lorraine Hansberry. Id. Osceola Macarthy Archer Adams. Osceola Archer Clipping File; Billy Rose Theatre Collection; New York Public Library for the Performing Arts, New York City.

p. 64. Bernice Johnson Reagon. *USA Today,* August 10, 1994. Ma Rainey. *Ma Rainey and the Classic Blues Singers,* by Derrick Stewart-Baxter. New York: Stein and Day, 1970.

p. 66. Eleanor Holmes Norton. Excerpt from a speech given at the American Bar Association, May 1974. Faye Wattleton. "Faye Wattleton Acceptance Speech: Humanist of the Year Award." *Humanist Magazine,* July/August 1986.

p. 66. Maria W. Stewart. Id.

p. 67. Nikki Giovanni. *Black Feeling Black Talk/Judgement.* New York: William Morrow and Co., 1970.

p. 68. Fannie Lou Hamer. *Parting the Waters: America in the King Years 1954–1963,* by Taylor Branch. New York: Simon & Schuster, 1988. Harriet Tubman. Id.

p. 71. Charlotte Forten. *The Journal of Charlotte Forten,* ed. Ray Allen Billington. New York: Dryden Press, 1953. Mari Evans. *Black Women Writers (1950–1980): A Critical Evaluation,* ed. Mari Evans. Garden City, NY: Anchor/Doubleday, 1984.

p. 73. Nikki Giovanni. Dedication from *Those Who Ride the Night Winds.* New York: William Morrow & Co, 1983.

p. 74. Alice Childress. *Black Women Writers (1950–1980): A Critical Evaluation,* ed. Mari Evans. Garden City, NY: Anchor/Doubleday, 1984. Shirley Chisholm. *Unbought and Unbossed.* New York: Simon & Schuster Inc, 1970.

p. 75. Toni Cade Bambara. *Black Women Writers at Work: Conversations,* ed. Claudia Tate. New York: Continuum, 1983.

p. 76. Marian Wright Edelman. *The Measure of Our Success: A Letter to My Children and Yours.* New York: Beacon Press, 1992. Rosa Parks. *The Montgomery Bus Boycott and the Women Who Started It,* ed. Joanne Robinson. Knoxville, TN: University of Tennessee Press, 1988.

p. 79. Gwendolyn Brooks. *Report from Part One.* Id. Barbara Jordan. "An Interview with Barbara Jordan." *Senior Scholastic Magazine,* March 12, 1977.

p. 80. Margaret Walker. *How I Wrote Jubilee.* Detroit: Broadside Press, 1971. Frances Ellen Watkins Harper. *A Brighter Coming Day: A Frances Ellen Watkins Harper Reader,* ed. Frances Smith Foster. New York: Feminist Press, 1990.

p. 83. Angela Davis. *Woman, Race and Class.* New York: Random House, 1981. Jamaica Kincaid. "My Daughter's Home." *The New Yorker* magazine, December 19, 1988.

p. 84. Ma Rainey. From "Gone Daddy Blues." 1923. Lucille Clifton. *Black Women Writers (1950–1980): A Critical Evaluation,* ed. Mari Evans. Garden City, NY: Anchor/Doubleday, 1984.

p. 85. Zora Neale Hurston. *Dust Tracks on the Road.* Philadelphia: J.B. Lippincott, 1942. Ma Rainey. "Slave to the Blues." 1926.

p. 87. Pearl Bailey. "A Black Pearl." Interview in *The New York Times,* November 26, 1967. Terry McMillan. "McMillan's Millions," by Max Daniel. *The New York Times Magazine,* August 9, 1992.

p. 88. Coretta Scott King. *My Life With Martin Luther King.* New York: Doubleday & Co., 1969. Maria W. Stewart. Id.

p. 90. Mari Evans. *I Am a Black Woman.* New York: William Morrow & Co., 1970.